TOM JONES

A COMEDY ADAPTED BY

Jon Jory

FROM THE NOVEL BY HENRY FIELDING

Tom Jones (1st ed. - 11.26.12) - tomjones5es
Copyright © 2012 Jon Jory

The Rules in Brief

1) Do NOT perform this Play without obtaining prior permission from Playscripts, and without paying the required royalty.

2) Do NOT photocopy, scan, or otherwise duplicate any part of this book.

3) Do NOT alter the text of the Play, change a character's gender, delete any dialogue, cut any music, or alter any objectionable language, unless explicitly authorized by Playscripts.

4) DO provide the required credit to the author(s) and the required attribution to Playscripts in all programs and promotional literature associated with any performance of this Play.

For more details on these and other rules, see the opposite page.

Copyright Basics

This Play is protected by United States and international copyright law. These laws ensure that authors are rewarded for creating new and vital dramatic work, and protect them against theft and abuse of their work.

A play is a piece of property, fully owned by the author, just like a house or car. You must obtain permission to use this property, and must pay a royalty fee for the privilege—whether or not you charge an admission fee. Playscripts collects these required payments on behalf of the author.

Anyone who violates an author's copyright is liable as a copyright infringer under United States and international law. Playscripts and the author are entitled to institute legal action for any such infringement, which can subject the infringer to actual damages, statutory damages, and attorneys' fees. A court may impose statutory damages of up to $150,000 for willful copyright infringements. U.S. copyright law also provides for possible criminal sanctions. Visit the website of the U.S. Copyright Office (www.copyright.gov) for more information.

THE BOTTOM LINE: If you break copyright law, you are robbing a playwright and opening yourself to expensive legal action. Follow the rules, and when in doubt, ask us.

Playscripts, Inc.
450 Seventh Ave, Suite 809
New York, NY 10123

toll-free phone: 1-866-NEW-PLAY
email: info@playscripts.com
website: www.playscripts.com

Cast of Characters

MAN 1:
Allworthy
Black George
Servant
Maclachlan

MAN 2:
Tom

MAN 3:
Blifil
Curate
Lord Fellamar
Ensign Northington

MAN 4:
Squire Western
Doctor

MAN 5:
Thwackum
Mr. Fitzpatrick
Servant
Hangman

WOMAN 1:
Molly
Lady Bellaston
Landlady

WOMAN 2:
Deborah
Sophia

WOMAN 3:
Miss Bridget
Miss Western
Maid
Mrs. Fitzpatrick

WOMAN 4:
Jenny
Mrs. Waters
Maid

The play is designed for a cast of nine: five men, four women. It may be played by up to thirty if a larger ensemble is desirable.

Production Notes

The play is designed for fluid movement and furniture changes. All furniture changes are done by the cast, sometimes as a scene is in progress. The idea being that, almost without exception, the new scene begins immediately at the end of its predecessor. As to in-sight costume changes, they can be used or not used at the director's discretion. The furniture itself can look threadbare. Different furniture may be used for different locations or it can be all the same. The costumes, however, should be the best the budget can afford and bring color to the green-brown monochrome of the set. If the play is done with the specified nine actors there will need to be wardrobe help backstage as some change is almost always in progress. The play itself should run approximately 2 hours and 15 minutes with intermission.

A Brief Chat about Bawdry

There's no doubt about it, *Tom Jones* is an innocent's voyage to safe harbor through the storms of sexuality. It's rowdy, bawdy, charming, and delightful. As the adaptor, I understand that not all audiences will be comfortable with Tom, and I would rather a couple of lines were cut than Henry Fielding should not be enjoyed at all. You may red pencil the text (but not slash and burn) if that makes your production possible. I promise, as the adaptor, not to scream or faint.

TOM JONES
adapted by Jon Jory

FROM THE NOVEL BY HENRY FIELDING

ACT I

(An Elizabethan sort of stage but in a rustic style with hay bales scattered about. One possibility is the set could be made of them. There is a second level with stairs coming down from it. By each side of the stage stand makeup tables with mirror and lights for in-sight costume and wig changes. There are various ways to enter and leave the stage.)

WOMAN 1. *(Kissing a grown-up* TOM JONES:*)* Tom Jones was born for the pleasure of women and the consternation of men.

> *(*TOM *exits.* WOMAN 2 *tosses* WOMAN 1 *a doll. She cradles it.)*

WOMAN 2. He was born in the home of one Squire Allworthy to what might be called…

TOM. *(Re-enters. Ingenuous smile.)* Doubtful parentage.

> *(Exits.)*

ALLWORTHY. *(Enters.)* Squire Allworthy had been absent in London a full quarter year on very particular business.

> *(Exits.)*

WOMAN 2. He arrived late one evening and was greeted by…

WOMAN 3. Greetings brother.

WOMAN 2. His sister Bridget. The Squire's wife having died of…

> *(*WOMAN 4 *enters and immediately falls to the floor in a fit. She thrashes and dies.)*

WOMAN 2. Died of whatever that was.

ALLWORTHY. I am much fatigued by travel, sister, I'll retire to chamber. *(He walks the stage, enters his 'chamber,' where the doll has been placed on a hay bale.)* Blood of the lamb! An infant. Housekeeper!

> *(*WOMAN 2 *runs a circuitous route to his chamber, saying as she runs:)*

WOMAN 2. Mrs. Deborah Wilkins, servant of all work. In the fifty second year of a long life and never seen a man without his coat.

ALLWORTHY. *(Arrives and holds up the baby:)* What, Mrs. Deborah Wilkins, is this?

DEBORAH. Has the look of an infant, sir.

ALLWORTHY. Of course it's an infant. How comes it to my chamber?

DEBORAH. From some wicked strumpet sir, as has laid her sin at an honest man's door, and though your worship knows your own innocence, the world is censorious. *(Picks up the doll.)* Faugh! How it stinks. It doth not smell like a Christian. I say, Squire, put it in a basket and lay it at the churchwarden's door. It will or it won't live till morning.

ALLWORTHY. Indeed not. Care for the child tonight and in morning we must find it a wet nurse. The poor mother has done this to provide for the child and grateful I am she has not done worse.

WOMAN 4. A good man, surely.

ALLWORTHY. Sister!

> (BRIDGET *arrives.*)

I've a gift for you.

BRIDGET. An ornament for my person, brother?

> *(He hands her the child.)*

ALLWORTHY. Left by some poor woman to our care.

BRIDGET. It has a bright eye, the sweet babe. Your judgment?

ALLWORTHY. As I have no heir, I've a resolution to keep the child and breed him up as my own.

BRIDGET. I commend your charity brother.

DEBORAH. I say the unknown mother is an impudent slut, a wanton hussy, an audacious harlot, a wicked jade, and vile strumpet.

> (ALLWORTHY *exits. Lights change.* DEBORAH *and* BRIDGET *move downstage.* WOMAN 4 *is at the makeup table becoming* JENNY.)

So Miss, I've close scrutinized the characters of the young girls round about and fixed on Jenny Jones who the townsmen swarm like bees. I make her out the mother.

BRIDGET. Was she not nurse to me in my illness?

DEBORAH. She was that. The dirty slattern.

> *(Lights change. A chair is set.* JENNY *sits.* ALLWORTHY *enters to her.)*

ALLWORTHY. Jenny child, it is in my power as magistrate to punish you rigorously for you have laid your sins at my door. Truth, however, will be rewarded. Are you indeed the child's mother?

JENNY. Must I say?

ALLWORTHY. Whatever your answer you must leave the town. But the truth will give you fifty pounds to make your way in life.

JENNY. Then I will say I am.

ALLWORTHY. Be a good girl the rest of your days, for the greatest pleasure is an innocent and virtuous life. I will provide for the child in a better manner than you could ever hope. *(Gives her money.)* Safe travels girl. But Jenny, who is the father?

WOMAN 3. A question not to be answered till the end of the play, although it's completely irrelevant. We'll just say...

FULL CAST. Tom grew up!

(TOM enters grinning.)

WOMAN 1. And was, I'm afraid, no better than he should be.

WOMAN 2. And forever compared with Master Blifil.

WOMAN 4. Blifil...

(BLIFIL appears.)

Was the son of Bridget, the Squire's sister, and a Captain Blifil...

(Some male in the cast moves forward to stand with BRIDGET.)

Of whom we choose to say nothing. Bridget and the captain saw fit to die...

(They do.)

And Blifil was raised in the Squire's home as a companion to Tom.

WOMAN 1. He was in public an insufferable prig and in private...

(BLIFIL masturbates.)

THWACKUM. *(From the back of the stage:)* Stop that this instant!

WOMAN 2. Tom's abroad for an evening's shooting.

(Lights change.)

TOM. Black George!

BLACK GEORGE. *(Enters, having finished his makeup at a table.)* Eh, Tom?

TOM. *(Pointing:)* Quail in the thorn bush!

BLACK GEORGE. I'll clap em' and you blast em'.

(Moves toward a 'bush.' Claps hands. Bird flies. TOM *shoots.)*

True as a plum line, by God!

(Picks up dead bird that has fallen from above.)

Taint a quail, young'n, but a partridge.

SQUIRE WESTERN. *(Offstage:)* What devilment be this? What blackguards be poaching my property?!

BLACK GEORGE. Best run, Tom. *(Looks back:)* Tom!

(BLACK GEORGE exits as WESTERN *enters pointing a gun.)*

SQUIRE WESTERN. Deliver up, villain, or by God I'll core you like an apple!

TOM. It's Tom, Squire Western. Squire Allworthy's Tom.

WESTERN. Well, young Tom, you have trespassed my grounds and deceased my partridge. Speak, boy, who was it with you, for there were sure two shadows.

TOM. Only me, sir, and strayed to your property by honest mistake.

WESTERN. A man who mistakes by a quarter mile is a fool or a scoundrel. *(Grabs* TOM *by the ear.)* Squire Allworthy shall lash your mistake, sir.

(He drags a protesting TOM *in front of* ALLWORTHY *seated with* THWACKUM, *the tutor, and* BLIFIL *behind him.)*

ALLWORTHY. Since the boy's apprehension, Squire, tutor Thwackum has seen to a whipping.

THWACKUM. Twenty blows, Squire, ably given.

ALLWORTHY. Black George, my keeper, is sent from my service and Tom admits his part so mayn't we…

WESTERN. You drift toward pardon, sir. When a man shoots your partridge, Squire, he should repent in the stocks. You're a soft man sir, for we speak of poaching!

ALLWORTHY. A dozen partridges for your one, and see the matter done with.

WESTERN. A dozen you say?

THWACKUM. A bad example to master Blifil, Squire, who in every dealing reads the right from his bible.

BLIFIL. Always.

ALLWORTHY. Master Blifil knows therefore the uses of forgiveness. Twelve partridges and the matter settled.

WESTERN. On receipt of the birds, I shall say no more. *(Laughs.)* Twelve partridges for that boy is a fool's bargain!

    (Exits.)

ALLWORTHY. Go along Tom. No man is wise at all hours.

TOM. Oh sir, you're too good sir, I don't deserve it.

BLIFIL. Indeed you don't Tom, for it was three partridges, nor one.

    (TOM chases BLIFIL, giving him a resounding kick in the rear.)

ALLWORTHY. Tom, Master Blifil!

THWACKUM. For that you'll be whipped double, Thomas.

ALLWORTHY. *(Raising a hand:)* Tom may plead provocation. I dismiss this court and advise both lads to live more friendly and peaceable.

THWACKUM. Attend me Squire, I…

ALLWORTHY. You shan't whackem', Thwackum. Now, to our evening prayers.

    (ALLWORTHY, BLIFIL, and THWACKUM exit. TOM arrives in the woods at the shack of Black George. His daughter MOLLY sits before it.)

MOLLY. Well, chimes to heaven, if it ain't the young master. Been a good while, eh?

TOM. I come to see what might be done for Black George.

MOLLY. My father as is lost his position over a partridge, you mean?

TOM. I never told, Molly.

MOLLY. Did you not?

TOM. Never. He confessed to the squire.

MOLLY. Well he's drownin' his sorrows now and forever.

TOM. I brought him such monies as I have.

MOLLY. That'll do for him, but I'd need a kiss to forgive, young master.

TOM. Can't do that Molly. Not that I haven't thought of such.

    (She kisses him.)

MOLLY. Was it that you thought of?

TOM. Something like.

(She kisses him harder.)

MOLLY. Is that more like?

TOM. I must go.

MOLLY. Oh. Ow. There's a spider gone down the back of my dress. Ow. I'm bitten.

    *(*TOM *slaps the back of her dress.)*

Not that, Tom. Ow. Look down the back, can't you?

TOM. I can't be seen doing such.

MOLLY. Ow. Then step inside before I'm murdered.

    (She pulls him out of sight. The next dialogue is offstage.)

Have you found it?

TOM. Not yet.

MOLLY. Now can you see?

TOM. Oh. Oh!

MOLLY. You've found what you're looking for then?

TOM. Unexpected like.

MOLLY. I thought so.

    (Giggles. Lights change. TOM *enters followed by* MOLLY.*)*

So young Tom, do you feel forgiven now?

TOM. *(Agonized:)* What have I done?

MOLLY. Well, whatever it was I enjoyed it.

TOM. I lost track of myself it bein' so dark.

MOLLY. A maid has no defense against the violence of such passion.

TOM. *(Overtaken by guilt:)* Have I debauched you, Molly?

MOLLY. You have, yes. Do you love me, Tom?

TOM. Well, I must, mustn't I?

MOLLY. My father without a place and myself debauched. You wouldn't go to marrying such as me I suppose?

TOM. Well, as to that…

MOLLY. *(Decisive:)* Here's what's owed then. I mustn't starve must I? Now I seen you following the Western girl about like a tame cat.

TOM. Sophia, do you mean?

MOLLY. You must get me into service with her Tom. They say her maid's traipsed off to London town. That way I could earn the keep of myself and father. And I'd be nearby if the night was cold. You must ask her for me Tom. There's naught else you can do as a Christian man.

TOM. Well, I must, I suppose.

(MOLLY *leaps up with her legs around his waist.)*

MOLLY. Good lad. Shall we look for spiders?

(*Kisses him. The scene dissolves.* MOLLY *exits and* SOPHIA *enters.)*

SOPHIA. Was that you, Tom, calling across the garden?

TOM. It was, Miss Sophia.

SOPHIA. I'm very glad to see you again.

TOM. After the years in London I wondered would you know me?

SOPHIA. We played together as children, Tom.

TOM. Aye, we did that.

SOPHIA. Then why would I not remember?

TOM. Don't know. (*Holds out a caged bird.)* Welcome home, Miss.

SOPHIA. How sweet. What a pretty yellow. What sort is it?

TOM. A yellow bird, Miss.

SOPHIA. I shall give it the best of care, Tom. (*He doesn't leave.)* Was there anything else?

TOM. It's Black George, Miss. I got the poor fella to take me a'birding and shot, in error, Squire Western's partridge and Squire Allsworthy sent him off and he and his daughter left to starve.

SOPHIA. How very terrible.

TOM. She's a good girl to work, Molly is. Might you know, Miss Sophia, of a place to be had? Wouldn't matter how low. It's my fault she suffers as she does.

SOPHIA. Well… (*She considers.)* I've lost my maid, Beatrice, Tom. Would Molly suit, do you think?

TOM. Well, she's quick with clothes. I'm no judge for a Lady's Maid, Miss Sophie, but it would be the saving of the girl.

SOPHIA. Then you must send her and I will try.

(TOM *kneels and kisses her hand.)*

TOM. It's a great kindness, that is.

SOPHIA. *(Stepping back, embarrassed:)* Tomorrow then... For Molly.

(TOM *bows and exits.* SOPHIA *picks up the cage.*)

I shall call you Tommy, yellow bird. When no one's about.

(BLIFIL *enters.*)

BLIFIL. Miss Sophia, I was reading Corinthians and did not spy you out.

SOPHIA. Mr. Blifil, how...nice.

BLIFIL. What have we here imprisoned?

SOPHIA. A song bird, though I know not its kind. Tom gave it me.

BLIFIL. Did he? It is the Cocothrauster Respertiuus.

SOPHIA. Ah.

BLIFIL. Known for its undulating flight and unprepossessing appearance.

SOPHIA. Ah.

BLIFIL. Will you entrust the creature to me for a moment?

SOPHIA. You may take it by the small string on its leg but be ever so careful.

(BLIFIL *extracts the bird.*)

BLIFIL. I believe it's molting.

(BLIFIL *sets it free and it flies away.*)

SOPHIA. No! What have you done, Mr. Blifil.

BLIFIL. God's creatures should enjoy the liberty God provided.

SOPHIA. It has flown to the tree! You are malicious Master Blifil! How could you! Help!

TOM. *(Running in:)* What has happened, are you hurt?

SOPHIA. I...he...

TOM. Have you hurt her Blifil?

SOPHIA. He has released my dear bird for spite.

TOM. *(Chasing* BLIFIL:*)* You sir, shall be lodged in the tree as well!

SOPHIA. Tom.

TOM. Ha! You rascal.

SOPHIA. Tom!

(He stops.)

SOPHIA. Might the bird be brought down before it flies?

TOM. It shall, and at this moment. *(To* BLIFIL: *)* We shall speak further, Blifil.

(TOM runs to climb the tree as ALLWORTHY *and* THWACKUM *hurry on.)*

ALLWORTHY. What has happened, Miss Western?

SOPHIA. Master Blifil has driven off my pet bird against my wishes.

ALLWORTHY. *(To* BLIFIL:*)* Done what?

BLIFIL. Indeed Squire, I am very sorry for what I have done, but seeing the poor creature languished, I own I could not forbear giving it the freedom our Lord provides.

(There is a cry from offstage and then a splash.)

SOPHIA. Tom has fallen!

ALLWORTHY. Fallen?

THWACKUM. Young master seems to be bathing in the stream fully clothed.

SOPHIA. Go quickly for he may be injured!

(TOM, limping and soaked through, enters.)

TOM. No, I'm…quite well *(Shakes himself like a water dog.)* Yellow bird flew off just as I reached out.

SOPHIA. Oh no.

BLIFIL. *(Looking up:)* Dear, dear, a nasty hawk has carried it off.

(TOM smacks the back of his head.)

Ruffian!

WOMAN 4. We must here pause briefly while our hero divests himself of wetted dress.

(TOM onstage, is dressed and re-dressed in full sight. SOPHIA *remains on one side of him and* MOLLY *on the other.)*

There are those who will despise Tom Jones' behavior in the case of poor Molly and the ravishing Sophia. But we might recall that his affections were sequential. Having been struck…tutored, by Black George's daughter, he felt deeply that to debauch a young woman was a very heinous crime demanding he repent, though she was, of course, reputed one of the handsomest girls in the country. Lovely Sophia, a paragon of refined beauty, innocence, modesty, and sprightliness seemed far beyond his reach but anchored in his heart. Such, we must say, is no unusual dilemma in a young man's passage.

> (TOM *is now dressed dryly.* SOPHIA *and* WOMAN 4 *exit.* TOM *passes by* MOLLY.)

MOLLY. Hssst. A word, Tom Jones?

TOM. Out so late? Do you not attend Miss Sophia?

MOLLY. I knew you walked this way. *(Throws herself in his arms.)* Oh Tom, I've missed you terrible.

TOM. *(Trying to detach her:)* We shall be seen, Molly.

MOLLY. Lie down with me then.

TOM. We shall both be driven from our situations.

MOLLY. *(Having gotten him to the ground:)* I'm your Molly, Tom, never to be another's. D'ye love me?

TOM. I suppose I do.

MOLLY. Well, you must Tom, as I'm carrying your child.

TOM. What?

MOLLY. You'll stand to it, wontcha lad?

TOM. I suppose, but…

MOLLY. They shall drive me out at whips end. Oh, Tom, I've never done what we done.

TOM. I'm a terrible bad person, an't I Molly?

MOLLY. Best kiss and find out, Young Master.

> (*Scene changes.* SQUIRE WESTERN, *a* CURATE, *and* SOPHIA *present.*)

SQUIRE WESTERN. And is having a bastard all your news curate?

CURATE. The daughter of Black George I speak of, and quite at home here I regret to say.

SOPHIA. Is it Molly you speak of?

CURATE. The very same. I have counseled the girl, but gossips are at work.

WESTERN. Jones by creepers! It was he brought her to ye, eh Sophia? I smoke it! Zooks, but he's the father of the bastard, sure as tuppence.

CURATE. I should be sorry to hear he had done the devil's work.

WESTERN. Sorry? *(Roars with laughter.)* Dost pretend, curate, that though has never got a bastard?

CURATE. *(Avoiding the issue:)* I should be sorry the young gentleman should do himself injury in Squire Allworthy's opinion.

WESTERN. Hah! Allworthy loves a wench. He's as arrant a whore-master as any within five miles! Tom'll not suffer there, and the woman will like him the better for it. Eh, Sophy girl?

(WESTERN *and* SOPHIA *exit.* ALLWORTHY *enters and berates* TOM.)

ALLWORTHY. The girl I will not prosecute, sir, but you will attend me in my study for severe lectures and repair of your behavior.

(ALLWORTHY *exits. Lights change.* TOM *is alone.)*

TOM. *(Calling:)* Molly!

(MOLLY *enters in disordered dress.)*

MOLLY. Lor' Tom, it's midday, lad. We'll be prey to any passerby.

TOM. And you half-clothed.

MOLLY. I must rest for the child's sake, mustn't I.

TOM. I have come to speak of the fatal consequences that must attend our amour.

MOLLY. The what?

TOM. Squire Allworthy has strictly forbidden my ever seeing you more… *(She kisses him)* and discovery of such should end in my ruin and yours, thus… *(She kisses him.)* We must separate, Molly, which you must bear with resolution… *(She kisses his neck and down his chest)* but I will ever show the sincerity of my affection… *(She starts undoing his trousers)* by providing beyond expectation, which will soon lure a man to marry you.

MOLLY. *(Rising, outraged:)* And this is your love for me? All men are false! What signifies riches to my love? I cannot bear this!

THWACKUM. *(Stumbling out of Molly's shack in his underwear:)* What girl? Is the house ablaze?

TOM. Thwackum!

THWACKUM. Jones.

TOM. This is beyond wonderful.

THWACKUM. So sir, enjoy your mighty discovery and expose me at your pleasure. But it is you who have corrupted her innocence and I merely feast on the remains.

TOM. Expose thee? I was never better pleased with thee in thy life. Behave kindly to the girl and I shall never ope my lips. And you Molly, cleave tight to Thwackum and I will not only forgive your infidelity to me, but do you all the service I can.

    (Leaves whistling.)

MOLLY. *(Kicking* THWACKUM's *shins:)* I told thee to stay under the bed.

    *(*MOLLY *and* THWACKUM *exit.* SOPHIA *and* TOM *each side of the stage.* WOMAN 3 *center.)*

WOMAN 3. Though they spoke but little they now saw each other much and the charms of the incomparable Sophia…

    *(*SOPHIA *and* TOM *walk toward each other.)*

…the languishing softness of her eyes, the harmony of her voice and person. Her greatness of mind and sweetness of disposition…

    (They stop face to face.)

…conquered and enslaved the heart of poor Tom Jones and the God of love marched in, in triumph.

SOPHIA. Beautiful morning.

TOM. Very beautiful.

    (They step back.)

SOPHIA. I am mortified, Mr. Jones, that pursuing the dear bird, you fell from such a height. The water only preserved you from a severe fate.

TOM. Can you then desire me to live?

SOPHIA. How could I wish such a generous spirit ill?

TOM. *(Stepping to her within inches:)* This divine goodness is beyond every other charm.

SOPHIA. *(A weighted pause.)* I stay no longer.

    (Starts off.)

TOM. I have been unguarded.

SOPHIA. *(Stops.)* Yes.

TOM. One frown destroys me. You must blame your beauty. What am I saying? My heart overflows. I have struggled with my love to the utmost, concealing a fever which plays upon my vitals.

    (He kneels.)

SOPHIA. Mr. Jones! I will not effect to misunderstand you. Indeed I understand you too well. You must allow my way into the house. I wish I may be able to support myself thither.

> *(He takes her hand and kisses it.)*

Oh dear.

TOM. Oh mine.

> *(She exits, staggering. Lights down. Moon up.* TOM, BLIFIL, *and* THWACKUM *gather. Each carries a caudle.)*

THWACKUM. Young gentlemen, the news is dire. Squire Allworthy teeters on the black precipice of death.

TOM. It cannot be. We are bereft!

THWACKUM. It is the consumption.

BLIFIL. Of what acreage exactly is the property?

THWACKUM. Do not sorrow thus, dear boy. Death is the common lot in which the fortunes of all men agree.

TOM. The squire is all to me.

BLIFIL. He must not die before we have counted the plate and silver.

THWACKUM. I have the accounting. Let us say our farewells.

> *(As they circle the stage, the squire is brought on in a bed. A* DOCTOR, *in black, stands nearby.)*

ALLWORTHY. I have determined to speak a few words at this our parting.

> *(BLIFIL sobs.)*

THWACKUM. Poor Blifil, he loves you so.

ALLWORTHY. I leave you, Blifil, heir to my whole estate.

> *(BLIFIL falls to kissing him.)*

Pray leave me my last breath!

> *(THWACKUM yanks BLIFIL back.)*

ALLWORTHY. To you, Tom, five hundred pounds a year.

TOM. Oh, my friend, my father.

ALLWORTHY. And a thousand pounds to you, Thwackum.

THWACKUM. *(Thrilled:)* Five thousand pounds!

ALLWORTHY. One thousand.

THWACKUM. To make up six?!

ALLWORTHY. Clean out your ears, sir. You must leave me. I tire in discourse.

(BLIFIL *and* THWACKUM *go off.*)

THWACKUM. *(As they go:)* He said six quite clearly.

(ALLWORTHY *is cleared in the bed. The doctor and* TOM *are left alone.*)

TOM. I cannot bear, Doctor, to lose the squire.

DOCTOR. Ah, Mr. Jones, it was not my place to interrupt family matters, but I now have the satisfaction to say with assurance that the squire is out of danger.

(TOM *hugs and kisses the doctor.*)

TOM. Dear sir, next to the squire I love you of all men living! I must tell my Sophia.

(DOCTOR *exits.* TOM *spins in exaltation.*)

I will carve the squire's name in a thousand trees.

(MOLLY *appears.*)

MOLLY. Hello, Tom.

(*He turns holding the knife.*)

You wouldn't kill your Moll, would ya?

TOM. Why would I kill you, Molly Seagrem?

MOLLY. You've touched drink I see.

TOM. I have.

MOLLY. Give me your hand, Tom.

TOM. And why would you need that?

(*She places his hand on her breast.*)

MOLLY. So you might feel my hearts greeting.

WOMAN 4. *(Moving to the audience:)* Here evolved a parley we shall omit. It lasted a scant minute, at which juncture they retired to the thickest part of the grove.

(*They do.* THWACKUM *and* BLIFIL *enter.*)

THWACKUM. Man since the fall, Blifil, is but a sink of iniquity and a degradation of the flesh...that bush master, does it not seem... alive?

BLIFIL. Bush?

THWACKUM. Just there.

(Sounds of...well, romance.)

BLIFIL. And it speaks.

THWACKUM. *(Moving closer sees...)* Oh, fie upon it! Great thunderous balls! Is it you there, Jones?

TOM. Indeed, I am here and you are there.

THWACKUM. And who, sir, is that wicked slut?

TOM. You shall not know, sir, what wicked slut it might be.

THWACKUM. I Thwackum command you! The relation of master to scholar is indeniable, and you are, therefore, as much obliged to obey me now as when I taught you your first rudiments!

TOM. And the scholar informs you, you've a mountainous ass!

BLIFIL. *(Safely behind* THWACKUM:*)* I shall have you before the squire!

TOM. *(Chasing* BLIFIL:*)* And I shall have the tufts of hair from your empty head!

(While TOM *is thus engaged,* THWACKUM *attempts to pull* MOLLY *from the bush.)*

(TOM abandons the fallen BLIFIL, *who has assumed the fetal position, pulling* THWACKUM *back by the coat.* BLIFIL *fells* TOM *with a branch.* TOM *rising serves* BLIFIL *a fearful sock to the jaw, whereupon* THWACKUM *hits* TOM *with a book and* BLIFIL *tackles him.* SQUIRE WESTERN *on a walk with* SOPHIA *sees* TOM *getting the worst of it.)*

WESTERN. Two on one is it?

(Grabs THWACKUM *in a headlock.)*

There be no honor in such odds.

(TOM grabs BLIFIL *in a headlock. He and* WESTERN *face each other.)*

WESTERN. So it's you, young poacher!

TOM. It is I, sir.

WESTERN. Shall we rid ourselves of these gallants?

TOM. As you say squire.

(They back off and then run the heads in the headlocks together with great force. BLIFIL *and* THWACKUM *scream, and then zigzag and fall.* SOPHIA *screams and faints.* TOM *runs to her.)*

TOM. She is dead!

WESTERN. Tis naught but aladyfit, idjut.

TOM. Then I shall carry her to water, that she may revive.

(*Picks up* SOPHIA *and starts off.*)

WESTERN. Stream be t'uther way, lad.

(TOM *races in the other direction.*)

No, that be North. Back, stoutheart!

(TOM *reverses.*)

SOPHIA. Oh, heavens.

TOM. (*Stops.*) She speaks.

WESTERN. Well stand the lass down, crackbrain.

(*He does.*)

SOPHIA. Oh, father!

(*Moves to* WESTERN's *embrace.* BLIFIL *and* THWACKUM *have struggled to their feet.*)

WESTERN. (*To* TOM:) Gadzookers, sir! You thought only of my daughter, boy, and for such service there is naught but the lady and my hound, Slouch, you cannot have!

BLIFIL. The blackguard, having been discovered by us in a bush with a wench, has broken our heads.

WESTERN. What! Hast thou been tumbling a wench!

THWACKUM. Beat the bushes by the oak and there you shall find her.

WESTERN. (*Roars with laughter.*) Ah Tom, Tom, thou art a liquorish dog surely.

SOPHIA. I must go home, father.

WESTERN. Home then. But the whole company shall sup with me. I'd as soon rid the country of foxes as miss a good fight and the ale afterwards.

BLIFIL. I shall not sup with a man who has splitted my lip.

THWACKUM. And broke my spectacles. Come Blifil. There is comfort in prayer.

(*They exit.*)

SQUIRE WESTERN. Sour apples, eh? Is that you Molly Seagram? *(Pulling* MOLLY *from hiding:)* You shall sit to my right, girl. Nothing like a supple wench and a fair brawl to pique the appetite. *(Starts off.)* Come along, young conqueror!

> *(Lights change. A chair is set.* MISS WESTERN, *sister to* SQUIRE WESTERN, *enters.)*

SOPHIA. Auntie Western!

MISS WESTERN. Great news, Sophia. My brother, the squire, told me of your passion for a certain gentleman…no, no, no, you cannot hide it.

SOPHIA. I hide nothing, madam.

MISS WESTERN. Nonsense. We entirely approve.

SOPHIA. You do?

MISS WESTERN. And this very afternoon is appointed for you to receive your lover.

SOPHIA. Dear Aunt, you frighten me out of my senses.

MISS WESTERN. Pooh, my dear. His perfections suit admirably.

> *(SOPHIA embraces her.)*

Now, now.

SOPHIA. I had not hoped! I own, Aunt, I know none so brave, gentle, and handsome. What signifies his being base born, when compared with such qualifications as these.

MISS WESTERN. Mr. Blifil base born?

SOPHIA. Blifil?

MISS WESTERN. Of whom else have we been speaking?

SOPHIA. Good heavens! Of Mr. Jones and no other.

MISS WESTERN. You would think of allying yourself to a bastard? Can the blood of the Westerns submit to such contamination? *(Calling:)* Mr. Western!

> *(SOPHIA sits furious.)*

Mr. Western, I say!

WESTERN. *(Enters.)* Am I called for like a summer hay bundler?

MISS WESTERN. She will not have Blifil, sir.

WESTERN. *(To* SOPHIA:*)* Not have Blifil? *(To* MISS WESTERN:*)* Not have Blifil! *(Pounding his fist:)* Blifil is the man!

SOPHIA. Father, don't make me the most miserable creature on earth by forcing me to marry a man I detest. It would be the death of me.

WESTERN. Detest'un never so much, you shall have un! Without consent I will not support you a farthing. No, though I saw you expiring on the street I would not vouchsafe a morsel of bread. Blifil, Blifil, and Blifil it will be!

(Leaves the room only to run forcibly into TOM.)

Watch your way, sir.

TOM. I have heard that Blifil is proposed…

WESTERN. Through the keyhole, sir?

TOM. I bent down for a fallen coin, Squire.

WESTERN. It shall be Blifil!

TOM. A better match could not be found, squire. May I go in to your daughter and endeavor to obtain her concurrence with your inclination?

WESTERN. *(Stunned:)* Really?

TOM. Absolutely.

WESTERN. Good fellow, sir! Prithee try what thou canst do, lest I turn the wench out of doors. Miss Western!

(She follows WESTERN out, looking suspiciously at TOM. TOM and weeping SOPHIA are left alone.)

TOM. Do not weep, Sophia, I cannot bear the dreadful sound.

SOPHIA. Oh, Mr. Jones, you know not…

TOM. I know all… Your father sends me as advocate for my odious rival. O, promise me you will never give yourself to Blifil?

SOPHIA. Never.

TOM. Then may I hope?

SOPHIA. Mr. Jones, whither will you drive me? What hope have I to bestow? I would ruin both myself and you should I comply with your desire.

(WESTERN has tiptoed back and listens at the door.)

You must fly from me forever.

TOM. Indeed I can never part with you, indeed I cannot.

(SOPHIA throws herself into his arms.)

SOPHIA. Oh, Tom.

> (WESTERN *explodes into the room.*)

WESTERN. Thou inglorious wenchsnatch!

> (SOPHIA *faints in* TOM's *arms.*)

TOM. I will not, squire, be provoked to lift my hand against the father of Sophia.

> (*Hands him the fainted* SOPHIA.)

We shall settle when you are less wroth.

> (TOM *exits.* SOPHIA *exits. A writing desk is set for* ALLWORTHY. WESTERN *enters banging his fist on the desk.*)

ALLWORTHY. Squire Western?

WESTERN. My daughter has fallen in love with your bastard. This comes, sir, of breeding up a mongrel as a gentleman.

ALLWORTHY. I am heartily sorry, Western.

WESTERN. A pox on your sorrow.

ALLWORTHY. Well, what, squire, would you have me do on such an occasion?

WESTERN. Keep the damned rascal away from my house! She shall marry Blifil and if I catch Tom Jones, I will qualify him to run for the Geldings plate!

> (*He storms out. Lights change.* ALLWORTHY *talks to* BLIFIL.)

BLIFIL. How may I further consider a Christian woman who affects such a blackguard? I know him to be the worst man in the world.

ALLWORTHY. Is there more than I know, Blifil?

BLIFIL. When you were ill, sir, on the very day of your utmost danger, and we all in tears, he filled the house with riot and debauchery, and when reprimanded he struck me full upon the lip thus.

ALLWORTHY. Such goodness in concealing such villainy!

> (*Lights change.* ALLWORTHY *berates* TOM *to* BLIFIL's *immense pleasure.*)

I say guilty, sir. I have forgiven you too often in hope of amendment. Steal away Sophia, tumble a wench in my fields, pummel the lip of good Blifil? You must quit my house, sir.

TOM. I promise, Sir, that…

ALLWORTHY. I will not turn you naked into the world. You will find in this paper a small beginning and letter which with industry may secure you an honest livelihood. Leave my house on the moment!

TOM. But squire…

ALLWORTHY. Not another word!

> (ALLWORTHY *departs.* TOM *sits on the ground and writes a letter.*)

TOM. My Sophia: I have resolved to fly forever from your dear sight. You must think I never loved you or deserved you. I can say no more. My tears erase the words.

SOPHIA. (*Elsewhere on stage writes in return:*) It is impossible to express what I feel; but believe this, that nothing but the last violence shall ever give my hand or heart where you would be sorry to see them bestowed.

TOM. (*Rising:*) I shall leave this house tonight.

SOPHIA. (*Rising:*) I shall leave this house tonight.

> (SOPHIA *exits.* TOM *is given a pack for the road. Moonlight.*)

MOLLY. (*Suddenly appearing:*) Tom. Where are you…

TOM. I am exiled on Blifil's testimony. The Squire has given me a beginning in this paper.

MOLLY. How much Tom?

TOM. Haven't looked.

MOLLY. How I will miss you. (*Touching her own breasts:*) I shall always remember you…here.

TOM. I shall remember you there as well, Molly.

MOLLY. Shall we…

TOM. I've no heart for it.

MOLLY. One kiss then.

> (*They embrace. Passion grows. He pulls away.*)

TOM. Goodbye Molly.

MOLLY. Godspeed, Tom Jones.

> (*He exits. From behind her back she produces* ALLWORTHY's *letter.*)

Two hundred pounds!

(She dances a fierce jig and exits. The forest lights change. It is day and TOM *tramps along.)*

WOMAN 3. *(Runs on.)* Two days later. Or three. Whichever.

(Runs off. We hear screaming off. TOM *rushes toward the sound and returns immediately fighting* ENSIGN NORTHINGTON *with a sword, and he armed only with his walking stick.* MRS. WATERS *enters, stripped to her corset.* TOM *prevails and sends his adversary flying.)*

MRS. WATERS. My savior, do not pursue him and leave me solitary in this forest.

TOM. *(Bowing:)* Tom Jones, your ladyship.

MRS. WATERS. Mrs. Waters, Sir. Pray forgive my dishabille.

TOM. You must not kneel, madam. For you shall be…chilled.

MRS. WATERS. Are you man or angel?

TOM. Man, certainly. Is there a place nearby where you might procure dress?

MRS. WATERS. I am abandoned here, stranger to my surroundings.

TOM. The town nearest is Upton, I think. There, I am sure, we may furnish you all manner of convenience.

MRS. WATERS. Will you accompany me sir, that I may not be further preyed upon.

TOM. What villain has treated you thus?

MRS. WATERS. I had absconded my husband's ill treatment under protection of an ensign Northerton, but he, finding me in possession of jewels and coin, attacked me as he did you, tearing my dress and attempting to hang me by my garter!

TOM. Your own garter?! I find I have beaten him insufficiently. I will follow the scoundrel.

MRS. WATERS. Stay, handsome sir. To Upton, I beg you. Oh. My nakedness I see discomposes.

TOM. I will walk before you, lest my eyes offend.

MRS. WATERS. But sir…

TOM. I cannot answer for my power of resisting the charms of so much beauty.

MRS. WATERS. *(Fully aware:)* I am not aware.

TOM. You must take my coat.

MRS. WATERS. You must put it on me. *(He does.)* Your hands are warm.

> (TOM *removes them as if scalded.*)

WOMAN 3. *(Runs on.)* The inn at…whew…Upton. *(Looks off:)* Oh God.

> *(Runs off.)*

TOM. Landlord!

LANDLADY. At your service, young gentlemen.

TOM. Two rooms, landlady.

LANDLADY. For you sir, by all means. The beggar wench shall stay below stairs.

MRS. WATERS. Do you impugn my virtue, you calamitous, untutored, mongrel bitch?!

LANDLADY. *(Curtsying:)* You have convinced me of your virtue. Two rooms are yours at the top of the stairs.

> *(She exits. A table is placed.* MRS. WATERS *and* TOM *eat by candlelight.)*

TOM. How do you find the roasted beef, Mrs. Waters?

MRS. WATERS. The beef, sir, has my full attention.

TOM. And the quality of the ale?

MRS. WATERS. It has, Mr. Jones, my tongue in a dither.

TOM. I see.

MRS. WATERS. Might you share with me this voluptuous peach?

TOM. I cannot refuse.

> *(She takes a bite. He takes a bite. They eat simultaneously with many 'm-m-m-m's.)*

MRS. WATERS. You have left a drop of nectar at the corner of your lip. Allow me to expunge it. *(She delicately licks it away. Her napkin, covering her chest falls away.)* Oh. I am exposed.

TOM. You are… it is…they are.

MRS. WATERS. Fair conqueror, the fruits of victory are yours. *(Grabs him by the hair and pulls him to her.)* Come here, my beauty.

WOMAN 3. *(Running on:)* We must here interrupt events you may well imagine. Such foibles and vices you would not, I am sure wish represented. Would you? Of course not, thus we declare an interval for...well, for wholesome food, wholesome thought and...watering... as might be needed.

(She curtsies.)

Gentleman. Ladies. A quarter hour.

(She runs off and the house lights come up.)

End of Act I

ACT II

(Lights up on WOMAN 3.*)*

WOMAN 3. Only lost a few, thank Thespis. Now…while Tom and Mrs. Waters…conversed, there arrived by coach a Mrs. Fitzpatrick.

*(*MRS. FITZPATRICK *enters.* WOMAN 3 *exits.)*

MRS. FITZPATRICK. Innkeeper!

LANDLADY. My lady?

MRS. FITZPATRICK. I am Mrs. Fitzpatrick. My husband pursues me for an imagined wrong. I ask as one woman to another that you place me from harm's way.

LANDLADY. I'll have no hulabaloo here, mistress. No ruckus, no riot, nor the devils handwork.

MRS. FITZPATRICK. This necklace for your assistance.

LANDLADY. Done. I've a room occupied by a single gentleman otherwise engaged in the room of a traveling strumpet. This you may safely occupy as he's occupied elsewhere.

MR. FITZPATRICK. *(Enters.)* Landlord.

MRS. FITZPATRICK. Hurry! *(She is conducted to* TOM's *room.)*

MR. FITZPATRICK. Landlord, I say!

LANDLADY. There ain't two of me, is there.

(She rushes down.)

MR. FITZPATRICK. You're a woman.

LANDLADY. My husband was recently taken by lightning strike, sir, looked like roast beef, so you may address all inquiries to me.

MR. FITZPATRICK. Be there a lady in the house? For I have misplaced my wife and I come in armed pursuit of her.

LANDLADY. There is a woman of rude behavior taken a room, sir.

MR. FITZPATRICK. Alone or in company?

LANDLADY. That, sir, a Christian lady may not say, sir.

MR. FITZPATRICK. Take me to this creature!

(During their scene a bed has rolled on containing TOM *and* MRS. WATERS. *A doorframe is set. The* LANDLADY *and* FITZPATRICK *arrive at the room. He pounds on the door.)*

MR. FITZPATRICK. I have come to collect you, woman!

MRS. WATERS. Ensign Northerton!

(FITZPATRICK *kicks the door open.* TOM *leaps out of bed.*)

TOM. Declare yourself, sir!

(MRS. WATERS *hides under the covers.*)

MR. FITZPATRICK. *(Seeing* MRS. WATERS' *clothes on the floor:)* I am James Giric Eochaid Fitzpatrick. And whose ribbons, petticoats, stays and garters are these, sir?

TOM. Said ribbons, petticoats, stays and garters have naught to do with you, sir.

MR. FITZPATRICK. Only in so far as I must kill you, sir.

WOMAN 1. *(Enters and freezes the action.)* One moment! *(To the audience:)* Now next to this riotous chamber was deposited, in sleep, a caballero or cavalier, arrived too early for introduction. Hearing a woman's cries, he leapt from his bolster, took up his sword and flew to defend the afflicted.

(MR. MACLACHLAN, *as you will hear him called, joins the fray.*)

MR. MACLACHLAN. Hold villains or die by a swordsman's prick. *(He reconsiders.)* Rather, die from the prick of a swordsman's sword.

TOM. I choose the second.

(TOM *and* MACLACHLAN *fight.*)

MR. FITZPATRICK. Leave him to me, sir!

MACLACHLAN. A frog up your nose, sir!

(MACLACHLAN *and* FITZPATRICK *fight.*)

MACLACHLAN. Fitzpatrick?

FITZPATRICK. Maclachlan?

BOTH. Old School Fellow!

FITZPATRICK. I am rejoiced to see you. *(Points to* TOM.) This fellow hath debauched my wife.

MACLACHLAN. Barbarous. We shall spit him like a piglet.

(Both fight TOM.)

MRS. WATERS. *(Appearing from under the covers:)* Murder, robbery, rape!

MACLACHLAN. *(Seeing her:)* Wait! Do I not know Mrs. Fitzpatrick well and do I not see this lady is none of her?

FITZPATRICK. Oh. Pardon. You are stouter than my wife, and older.

MRS. WATERS. What?!

MACLACHLAN. Indeed Mr. Fitzpatrick, it is a shame to disturb a man and woman innocently coupling.

MRS. WATERS. You disgrace me, sir. This gentleman...

    (Indicates to TOM.)

TOM. Ran to the lady's assistance believing she had been set upon by robbers.

LANDLADY. I harbor no highwaymen here.

TOM. I must apologize to the lady for appearing before her in my shirt only.

MRS. WATERS. Accepted. I appreciated the use of your sword, sir.

TOM. It was a pleasure to labor with it on your behalf.

FITZPATRICK and MACLACHLAN. Our deepest regrets.

MRS. WATERS. In future gentlemen, you should look before you leap.

FITZPATRICK and MACLACHLAN. Many pardons. Goodnight.

MRS. WATERS. Goodnight.

TOM. *(To MRS. WATERS:)* Goodnight.

MRS. WATERS. Goodnight.

FITZPATRICK and MACLACHLAN. *(To TOM:)* Goodnight.

TOM. Goodnight.

FITZ and MAC. *(To each other:)* Goodnight.

    (They exit into the hall. TOM exits. As FITZPATRICK and MACLACHLAN converse, MRS. WATERS is rolled out and MRS. FITZPATRICK in.)

MR. MACLACHLAN. You must be weary from the road and our exertions. The inn being full, I suggest the sharing of my rooms and bed!

MR. FITZPATRICK. An honour, Maclachlan. I will tell you if I may, the tale of my wife's ingratitude, and her decamp.

    (They exit. TOM re-enters his room.)

TOM. Sleep. I must sleep. *(He pulls back the covers to find MRS. FITZPATRICK.)* Oh.

MRS. FITZPATRICK. Oh.

TOM. I must have the wrong room.

MRS. FITZPATRICK. Perhaps not.

TOM. Not?

MRS. FITZPATRICK. Perhaps.

TOM. *(Who doesn't:)* I see.

MRS. FITZPATRICK. I am unwarrantedly pursued by the very husband I heard challenge you in the next room. He is good humored in company but morose in marriage. I did not discern the dangerous fool through the disguise of gaiety and good breeding.

TOM. I understand madam, pray keep the room. I sleep well in a haystack.

MRS. FITZPATRICK. You will not, sir. It is I who trouble you. Place your sword between us on the bed, as was common with knights of old, and we will pass the time quite chastely.

TOM. I am tired.

MRS. FITZPATRICK. Your sword, sir. *(TOM places it.)* Now blow out the candle and we will speak no more.

    (TOM blows out the candle.)

TOM. Oh. Terribly sorry.

MRS. FITZPATRICK. Of course. *(Silence.)* Oh!

TOM. I was only...

MRS. FITZPATRICK. Oh! Oh yes! Oh yes! *(Silence.)* How very nice.

    (SOPHIA, running away, arrives at the Inn.)

SOPHIA. *(Tentatively:)* Landlord?

LANDLADY. Your ladyship?

SOPHIA. Are you...

LANDLADY. My husband was quite severed by lightning, m'lady. I was not expecting at this hour. The inn is full I fear.

SOPHIA. I will warm myself, if you will allow me, and then ride on.

LANDLADY. I may not hear of it. Step in, for I have mutton of all kinds and a bearable chicken.

SOPHIA. I am resolved to be on horseback again in three hours.

LANDLADY. My best rooms are let to contentious gentlemen and the next to a nasty trull and a Mr. Jones.

SOPHIA. Mr. Jones! I…is he a handsome young gentlemen?

LANDLADY. That I'll grant him.

SOPHIA. A small scar here?

(LANDLADY nods.)

But surely you are mistaken to say he is accompanied?

LANDLADY. Oh, I see. Come this way m'lady, you shall behold the doing with your own eyes.

(They go to TOM's room where he lies with MRS. FITZPATRICK.)

Are you sure, m'lady?

(SOPHIA nods.)

Gentleman's naught but bears in the woods, Miss.

(Opens the door and is met with MRS. FITZPATRICK's shrieks.)

MRS. FITZPATRICK. What? Are you mad? We are occupied here!

(LANDLADY closes the door, SOPHIA having seen in.)

LANDLADY. Different lady, but there you have it.

SOPHIA. This breaks my heart. There is no world worth living in. I cannot stay.

(Rushes down to the front door, the LANDLADY trying to keep up. SOPHIA stops.)

Wait. Take this muff, the gentleman will know it well. *(Starts out again. Stops.)* I will write my name upon this scrap of paper. See it is conveyed to him that was once the world to me.

(Exits.)

WOMAN 1. The world suffered healing night to cover its wounds but as is often the case allowed the sun to rise on the morrow. Tom Jones woke with the light on the wrong side of his sword.

TOM. *(As near nakedness as decency allows.)* What? A muff and paper? This is Sophia's hand. Catastrophe! I…I must hire horses. *(Starts out.)* And clothe myself, of course.

(MR. MACLACHLAN and MR. FITZPATRICK enter.)

MR. MACLACHLAN. I tell you Fitzpatrick there was such bumping and rattling last night as I could not sleep.

MR. FITZPATRICK. I'm starving. Landlady?

(SQUIRE WESTERN enters.)

WESTERN. Landlord!

(TOM *enters now dressed.*)

TOM. Landlady!

MACLACHLAN and FITZPATRICK. You sir!

TOM. *(Seeing* SQUIRE WESTERN:*)* You sir!

SQUIRE WESTERN. *(Seeing* TOM:*)* You sir! Ha! I have cornered the dog fox and I warrant the bitch is not far off. *(Starts to* TOM:*)* My daughter's muff!

MR. FITZPATRICK. Whose muff?

SQUIRE WESTERN. Hast thou tumbled my daughter, poacher?

TOM. I swear Squire, I have never seen her.

MR. FITZPATRICK. Upon my conscience sir, you deny seeing the gentleman's daughter when you know I found you in her bed.

TOM. What?!

MR. FITZPATRICK. *(To* SQUIRE WESTERN:*)* I will conduct you sir where your daughter lies.

WESTERN. I shall feather the hussy like a sparrow.

TOM. No, wait…

(*They pound on* MRS. WATERS' *door.*)

MRS. WATERS. Who calls me thus?

(FITZPATRICK *opens the door.*)

MR. FITZPATRICK. Your daughter!

WESTERN. Beg pardon, madam. She is none of mine.

MRS. WATERS. Have I booked room in bedlam? For the lunatics are sure at large!

TOM. Squire Western, Miss Sophia is, even now, for London. Hearing I was here, she would not stay.

WESTERN. *(Clattering down to the front door:)* I must ride!

TOM. *(Racing out:)* As must I!

MACLACHLAN. Well, that was interesting.

MR. FITZPATRICK. Passed the time.

MRS. WATERS. *(Slipping her arms through those of both gentlemen:)* Gentlemen. As fate leaves me unaccompanied, I seek your protection and trust your honor on the road. On my part I will provide what delicate consolation a lady may offer to soften the cruel rigors of travel. Shall we go?

(Exeunt all. Lights change. We see SOPHIA *riding.* MRS. FITZPATRICK, *also riding, enters.)*

SOPHIA. Cousin!

MRS. FITZPATRICK. Cousin!

SOPHIA. Dearest Harriet, you meet me in flight from my father.

MRS. FITZPATRICK. And I from my husband. Your reason, cuz?

SOPHIA. For love.

MRS. FITZPATRICK. And I flee the disaster of having found it. Night falls. We must look about us, for women unaccompanied at dark are prey.

(Stray animal sounds.)

WOMAN 1. And so they rode until they saw...

MRS. FITZPATRICK. An Inn.

SOPHIA. An Inn.

WOMAN 1. An Inn.

MRS. FITZPATRICK. It looks to promise well. Tomorrow to London then.

SOPHIA. I'm aweary, cuz.

(Both women fall to the ground as if shot, and sleep.)

WOMAN 1. The sun, now being refreshed by sleep, did rise...as did...

(Both women rise from the ground.)

SOPHIA. Good morning, cuz.

MRS. FITZPATRICK. Good morning, cuz. Shall we to London then? *(The horses are strapped on.)* Shall we satisfy the tickle of our curiosity?

SOPHIA. My flight?

MRS. FITZPATRICK. And mine. Mr. Fitzpatrick was handsome, degage, gallant, and in his dress exceeded. But I soon found he preferred my money to my person.

SOPHIA. And your person so very fine...

MRS. FITZPATRICK. It is, yes. But it is easily imagined that when I once despised him I must consequently eschew his company, and thus I am in yours.

SOPHIA. Men are very confusing. I left my father's house for one, but apparently I was not sufficient.

MRS. FITZPATRICK. Men, dear Sophia, are swine. They swill you in and piss you out. Please forgive that in London I cannot offer you my hospitality for I will depend on the kindness of friends for my lodging.

SOPHIA. I had not thought. A lady Bellaston, dear friend to Squire Western's sister, will, I think, take me in.

WOMAN 4. Quite literally, we must fear.

     (SOPHIA *and* LADY FITZPATRICK *ride off.*)

Once in London town, Sophia directly found out the lady she sought.

     (LADY BELLASTON *enters.*)

For there was not a gentleman of refinement to whom Lady Bellaston was not…well known.

LADY BELLASTON. *(Addressing the audience:)* For beauty and wit are everywhere esteemed, and these I certainly possess.

WOMAN 4. And Sophia received, in return of her first inquiry, a most pressing invitation.

LADY BELLASTON. You must come to me tomorrow, child. And I will hook you up.

     (WOMAN 4 *does a double take at this contemporary phrase.* SOPHIA *and* MRS. FITZPATRICK *say their goodbyes.*)

SOPHIA. I can only recommend Miss Western's adage that when war is declared between husband and wife, she can hardly make a disadvantageous peace.

MRS. FITZPATRICK. And my advice, cuz, is to never give advice when in London, for it is always ill received.

     (*They wave goodbye with handkerchiefs.* MRS. FITZPATRICK *exits.*)

LADY BELLASTON. *(She takes* SOPHIA's *arm. They walk.)* I can easily clothe your radiant simplicity so you will have a dozen gentlemen hiding in your closets at once.

SOPHIA. But…

LADY BELLASTON. Not a word. I shall offer you every protection and see to your every pleasure.

(They exit. SQUIRE WESTERN *enters.)*

SQUIRE WESTERN. Lost the scent, damn me. Well, she shall suffer the most bitter execration good liquor may invent!

(He exits. TOM *and* MRS. FITZPATRICK *cross each other.)*

TOM. Mrs. Fitzpatrick?

MRS. FITZPATRICK. Mr. Jones, how unexpected.

TOM. Yes I… Well, I… You see…

MRS. FITZPATRICK. *(Rather enjoying his discomfort:)* Yes?

TOM. Miss Sophia.

MRS. FITZPATRICK. Ah.

TOM. I set forth each morning in pursuit of your cousin…

MRS. FITZPATRICK. Dear girl.

TOM. But many a weary step is to no better purpose than the one before it. Could it be my good fortune to find she is lodged with you?

MRS. FITZPATRICK. She is not. My residence is just there. Do not fail to visit should time and inclination converge. Oh. You needn't bring your sword.

(She exits. TOM *exits. A chair is set. A* MAID *brings tea.)*

MAID. Oh yes. My sister Bette is personal maid to Lady Bellaston where Miss Western lodges. She says the girl is forlorn in love with that Mr. Jones but discovered him in bed with a tart in Tottingham.

MRS. FITZPATRICK. A tart in Tottingham?!

MAID. Or two.

MRS. FITZPATRICK. If he be so terrible a rake, would be pity she should ever see him more.

MAID. Well, Lady Fitz, she says he's too pretty a man not to forgive.

MRS. FITZPATRICK. Is he? I didn't notice.

(The MAID *exits. Another chair is brought.* MRS. FITZPAT-RICK *and* LADY BELLASTON *sit talking.)*

LADY BELLASTON. And is this terrible man so well equipped a figure as he is represented?

MRS. FITZPATRICK. Simplicity of manner, and can be brought without undue trouble to the point.

LADY BELLASTON. I understand you.

MRS. FITZPATRICK. Of course you do.

LADY BELLASTON. Squire Western's sister hath described the Squire to be such a brute that I cannot consent to put any woman under his power who hath escaped from it. She shall be kept safe from Mr. Jones and immersed in the pleasures of gentlemen of quality.

MRS. FITZPATRICK. Mr. Jones may be left to me. He has threatened to call on me this very afternoon.

LADY BELLASTON. Oh? At what hour?

(MRS. FITZPATRICK *smiles and leaves without answering. Lights change.* TOM, MRS. FITZPATRICK, *and* LADY BELLASTON *converge from different directions.*)

MRS. FITZPATRICK. (*Not entirely happy to make the introduction:*) Mr. Jones, may I present the honorable Lady Bellaston.

(LADY BELLASTON *curtsies deeply.*)

LADY BELLASTON. You are very, very much, sir, as I have heard you described. What a happy accident that I happened to be passing.

(*Lights and furniture change.* TOM *is sitting alone in his lodgings, mending clothes. A female* SERVANT, *poorly dressed, enters.*)

SERVANT. (*Hands over a package:*) This here was delivered. I could mend these socks you know. You've hams for hands.

TOM. (*Taking them from the package:*) A domino, a mask, and a masquerade ticket. "The Queen of the fairies sends you this. Use her favors not amiss." Surely this is delivered in error.

SERVANT. You've cobblerocks for brains, don'cha? I make no doubt these was sent by a great lady you'll have the happiness of meeting at the masquerade.

TOM. But no lady knows my lodgings. Mrs. Fitzpatrick only. I believe she knows Sophia's whereabouts. By heavens, I shall be at the masquerade this evening!

(*A masked ball in progress. The full cast is engaged.* TOM *enters and dances with a* SHEPHERDESS. *A* LADY *approaches and speaks softly.*)

LADY. If you engage that trollop longer, I will acquaint Miss Western.

(*She moves away.* TOM *follows her.*)

TOM. Is she among the dancers then?

LADY. Hush sir, we will be observed. I promise you, upon my honor, Miss Western is not here.

TOM. Indeed, good fairy queen, I know you very well, your disguise notwithstanding. I beg, Mrs. Fitzpatrick, that you do not divert yourself by keeping Sophia from me.

LADY. And should I assist her ruin? The girl has nothing but what it pleases her father give her. Should you spoil her, he will give her nothing.

TOM. My love is not of that base kind. I would sacrifice everything to the possession of Sophia but Sophia herself.

LADY. And are you, sir, so little versed in the sex, to affront a lady by entertaining her with your passion for another? I say you must kiss my hand as a forfeit.

WOMAN 4. Tom had never less inclination to an amour than at present, but gallantry to the ladies was among his principles of honor. And he must accept a challenge to love as he would a challenge to fight.

LADY. 'Tis late, sir.

TOM. You must suffer me to see you home.

LADY. Are you used, Mr. Jones, to make these sudden conquests?

TOM. In no way, but as you have taken my heart by surprise, the rest of my body hath a right to follow.

    (The dance dissolves. A sofa and two chairs are set.)

LADY. *(Enters with* TOM.*)* I have a guest, fortunately at the theatre, what would she think of our being alone in each other's company at this time of night?

    (They kiss.)

TOM. I importune you, dear lady, to unmask.

LADY. That you may prefer my beauty to my kiss?

    (She unmasks.)

TOM. You are not Mrs. Fitzpatrick.

LADY BELLASTON. Some years younger, sir. Lady Bellaston desires your lips.

    (She kisses him.)

WOMAN 3. *(Steps in front of them.)* It would be tedious to continue the particular conversation and ordinary occurrences which lasted until six in the morning in Lady Bellaston's rooms. When all was thoroughly settled and a second meeting appointed, they separated.

(They do, a few paces.)

The next evening Tom Jones arrived as appointed.

(They return to their lovemaking.)

And the usual civilities accrued. *(She looks behind her.)* However, I am far from desiring to exhibit such pictures to the public as may be set forth in French novels, available only in bad translations.

LADY BELLASTON. Tomorrow, dear boy…no, Wednesday…perhaps both. But use my private stair.

(The furniture departs as does the LADY. TOM *is now dressed in finery by the cast.)*

WOMAN 3. Lady Bellaston's violent fondness we can no longer conceal and by her means Tom was now raised to a state of affluence beyond any he had ever known.

TOM. This state of affluence is beyond any I have ever known. But nothing is more irksome, I think, than to repay love with gratitude. *(He is handed a letter.)* "Come to me exactly at seven. I dine abroad but will come to you. If it would amuse you, you may use the front door."

(A chair is set. A SERVANT *speaks to* TOM.)

SERVANT. I'm sorry, sir, her ladyship instructed you might be admitted only at the stroke of seven.

TOM. And I say, bother the quarter of an hour.

(He brushes past and sees SOPHIA *arranging her hair in an imaginary mirror downstage. After a moment she sees him behind her in mirror.)*

SOPHIA. Oh!

TOM. Oh!

SOPHIA. Dear heaven! I almost doubt whether you are the person you seem.

TOM. Indeed I am that very wretched man.

SOPHIA. I must…

TOM. Let us not, I beseech you, lose these precious moments which fortune has so kindly sent us. On my knees, let me ask you pardon.

SOPHIA. But you cannot expect…after your…

TOM. I know. No less than unforgivable. That cursed Inn! That was not love, Sophia.

SOPHIA. To have my name traduced among the vulgar in a public place.

TOM. This is your charge? I swear I never spoke your sacred name in such as that.

SOPHIA. Have you not?

TOM. Not. It is an offense utterly foreign to my character.

SOPHIA. *(Thinking carefully:)* All else I might…forgive.

TOM. Then would you…might you…

SOPHIA. I would but I cannot. Did not my duty, which I have now reclaimed, forbid me to follow my own inclinations, ruin with you would be more welcome than fortune with another.

TOM. *(Agonized:)* Ruin, Sophia? Your words destroy me. *(Pounds himself with his fists.)* I shall never act so base a part! I shall carry this love to some rocky promontory, foreign to man; from whence no voice, no sigh of my despair shall ever reach you. And when I am dead…

> *(She stops his mouth with a kiss, then suddenly backs away.)*

SOPHIA. But…

TOM. But what?

SOPHIA. *(Looking around her:)* But how…

TOM. How what?

SOPHIA. How came you to be…here?

TOM. Here? Oh, you mean here?

SOPHIA. This room. This residence?

TOM. Yes…here. I…am here…because…

> *(LADY BELLASTON enters. Sees TOM and SOPHIA. Collects herself.)*

TOM. You mean here?

SOPHIA. *(Seeing her:)* Lady Bellaston.

TOM. *(Seeing her:)* Ah.

LADY BELLASTON. I thought, Miss Western, you had been at the play?

SOPHIA. But it was so dreadful…all brigands and life in the stews, so at the interval I returned.

LADY BELLASTON. Of course you did, my dear. I should not have broken in so abruptly, Miss Western, had I known there was a gentleman.

SOPHIA. The gentleman is but a childhood friend.

LADY BELLASTON. And a very pretty friend indeed.

TOM. A pleasure, my lady.

LADY BELLASTON. Lady Bellaston. How amusing, I have never pronounced my own name before. How fortunate that you found her here, for it is very little known.

TOM. Madam, it is by the luckiest chance imaginable I made the discovery. I mentioned Miss Sophia to a lady at the masquerade ball who informed me I might find Miss Western here. I came at the first possible moment, asked for your ladyship and being told you would appear on the stroke of seven was shown into this room where I found Miss Western returned from the play.

LADY BELLASTON. Very neatly explained.

TOM. Was it not? Well, I must…leave you, with one request only, that I may be permitted the honor of another visit?

LADY BELLASTON. Would you like that Sophia?

(SOPHIA *nods energetically.*)

Sir, I see by your dress that you are a gentleman and my doors are never shut to people of fashion.

(TOM *bows to both ladies and departs.*)

Quite delectable, do you not think?

SOPHIA. Did he not seem awkward, even ungentle?

LADY BELLASTON. Did he? I will give orders that we are not at home to him.

SOPHIA. But there was an elegance in his awkwardness.

LADY BELLASTON. You blush, dear. You must forgive me, Sophia, but since he omitted his name, I suspicioned he might be the Mr. Jones your father so execrates.

SOPHIA. *(Forcing a laugh:)* Really? Did you?

LADY BELLASTON. But as you have promised never to marry without your father's consent, you would not be so ignoble as to keep company with the fellow.

SOPHIA. Upon my honor, madam. That Mr. Jones is as entirely indifferent to me as the gentleman who just left us.

LADY BELLASTON. *(Kissing* SOPHIA *on the cheek:)* Well then, perhaps I shall have him.

(She exits, then SOPHIA.*)*

*(*TOM's *lodgings.* TOM *sits. The* MAID *appears.)*

MAID. Letter from a lady of fashion, sir. Seems to fancy you as I read it. *(She exits.)*

TOM. *(Reads:)* "When you left the room, I little imagined you would leave my house. Please return to me the clothes…and all they contain." Lord help me.

MAID. *(Enters.)* Second note. Same lady. *(Exits.)*

TOM. *(Reading:)* "My letter was too warm. I must, and will, see you tonight." What may a man do?

(LADY BELLASTON bursts in. Kisses TOM.*)*

LADY BELLASTON. You see sir, when women have gone one length too far, they will stop at nothing. *(Slaps him.)* Have you betrayed my honor to her?

TOM. The maid is coming. Hide in the closet.

(LADY BELLASTON does.)

MAID. Got her in the closet have you?

(Gives him tea and exits. LADY BELLASTON *pops out.)*

LADY BELLASTON. Honor and reputation lost. Your letter to Sophia intercepted. Oh, I should kill you, sir…but will relent if you'll disrobe. *(Starts undressing.)* You may come to me at seven, for gossip will suppose you to visit your Sophia, but your reward, sir, will not come from her.

*(*TOM *puts his head in his hands. The scene freezes.* LADY BELLASTON *exits. The* MAID *enters.)*

MAID. Well, that didn't take long. Letter from your other bit.

(Exits. SOPHIA *enters and speaks the following letter as* TOM *reads.)*

SOPHIA. Sir, it is impossible to express what I have suffered since you left this house. Lady Bellaston is, I think, in some suspicion. If you have any concern for my ease do not return hither.

(She exits.)

TOM. I must see Sophia at any cost!

    (He exits. MAID *enters.)*

MAID. The cock flown, and I haven't had my turn yet.

    (She exits. LADY BELLASTON *and* LORD FELLAMAR, *a young nobleman, enter talking.)*

LADY BELLASTON. So, my agreeable lord, what do you make of the girl?

LORD FELLAMAR. A goddess, lady. Who is this blazing star you have produced among us?

LADY BELLASTON. This blazing star, Lord Fellamar, is the daughter of a country booby and in London for the first time.

LORD FELLAMAR. Impossible. I should swear she had been bred up in court. I am in love with her quite to distraction.

LADY BELLASTON. An only child and her father's estate is three thousand pounds a year.

LORD FELLAMAR. Then I think her the best match in England.

LADY BELLASTON. And I sire, heartily wish you had her.

LORD FELLAMAR. And will.

LADY BELLASTON. But you have a rival my Lord Fellamar.

LORD FELLAMAR. You have struck a damp to my heart.

LADY BELLASTON. A beggar, a bastard, a foundling, and lower than one of your lordship's footmen.

LORD FELLAMAR. Such a sleek mare must only be bred to quality.

LADY BELLASTON. Youth cannot be reasoned from folly. She may flee to the boy at any time, thus only violent methods will do, you understand me?

LORD FELLAMAR. Blast! For the reeling in, as you know well, is the better part of the pleasure.

LADY BELLASTON. Dine here today and I will place her in your charge.

LORD FELLAMAR. Without preamble?

LADY BELLASTON. You must gird up, Lord Fellamar. You know the tale of the Sabine Ladies who, though forced, make tolerable good wives afterwards. She is the most delicious girl, that's certain.

LORD FELLAMAR. Oh very well, she shall be mine within the time you give.

*(*LADY BELLASTON *exits. Lights change.* SOPHIA *enters.)*

SOPHIA. I own sir, I am surprised at this unexpected visit.

LORD FELLAMAR. Surely, goddess, you could not detain my heart in your possession without receiving a visit from its owner.

(He encircles her waist.)

SOPHIA. Am I really to conceive your lordship to be out of his senses?

LORD FELLAMAR. Quite in my senses. Forgive me, for I cannot live, nor will I live without you.

(She breaks his hold and slaps him.)

How very enjoyable.

SOPHIA. I will scream, sir.

LORD FELLAMAR. The house is empty and cannot hear. This be the only way my despair points me.

(He forces her to the ground and we hear…)

SQUIRE WESTERN. Where is she? Damn me if she shan't be unkenneled this instant.

(He enters and sees FELLAMAR *wrestling with* SOPHIA.*)*

LORD FELLAMAR. You have scratched me, cat. *(Grabs* SOPHIA *by the throat.)*

WESTERN. What, villain, do you lay hands upon my daughter? *(Pulls* FELLAMAR *up and fells him with a blow.)* Now, who the devil are you?

LORD FELLAMAR. *(Groggily rising:)* I am Lord Fellamar, sir, the happy man you will honor by accepting me for a son-in-law.

WESTERN. *(Grabbing him by the collar:)* You are a son-of-a-whore and be damned to you!

LORD FELLAMAR. I cannot hear such language without resentment.

WESTERN. Resent my ass. I'll lick thy jacket!

*(*LADY BELLASTON *enters.)*

LADY BELLASTON. Squire Western.

(He lets go of FELLAMAR.*)*

Lord Fellamar.

LORD FELLAMAR. Your ladyship. *(To* WESTERN:*)* I shall no more pummel you before the ladies.

SQUIRE WESTERN. *(Chasing him:)* Shall you not?

SOPHIA. Let him go, father.

LADY BELLASTON. *(Patting SOPHIA's hand:)* Were the children teasing?

LORD FELLAMAR. *(Trying to straighten his clothing:)* I fear I am expected at my club. *(To WESTERN:)* Your humble servant, sir. *(To SOPHIA:)* Mademoiselle and Lady Bellaston, your most obedient.

    (He flees.)

LADY BELLASTON. Bless me sir, what have you done? He is a nobleman of great rank and fortune and has condescended to propose to your daughter his hand in marriage.

WESTERN. Condescended! My Sophy shall have an honest country gentleman. I have pinched one for her, and she shall have'un. *(Pulling SOPHIA by the hand:)* Come girl. *(Pulling her off:)* Your Lord, Lady Bellaston, is naught but a rutting goose.

    (They exit.)

LADY BELLASTON. *(Alone:)* What you begin, Lord Fellamar, you must finish!

    (She exits. TOM enters and stops dead in mid-stride.)

TOM. Perhaps…indeed! The only sure way to rid myself of the lady is to propose marriage, for no lady of fashion would submit to become a wife. I must venture or be lost forever.

    (He circles the stage while furniture is set. LADY BELLASTON and TOM enter simultaneously.)

LADY BELLASTON. An unexpected pleasure sir, as I have not seen or heard from you all day, but do not think I mean to scold you; for I never will give you excuse for the cold behavior of a husband by putting on the ill humor of a wife.

TOM. You have given me my cue and I must take it. *(He kneels.)* My sole ambition is to have the glory of laying my liberty at your feet so you may bestow on me a legal right to call you mine forever.

LADY BELLASTON. You jest, sir.

TOM. Never less, m'lady.

LADY BELLASTON. Yours forever! Do you fancy yourself capable of persuading me out of my senses? What? Deliver my whole fortune into the power of a muddy bumpkin that he might support his hounds at my expense? Am I mistaken for a serving girl? A wife, sir? I am…dismayed.

(She faints.)

TOM. She will not have me!

(An 18th-century end zone dance and then…)

LADY BELLASTON. Marriage is naught but servitude sir, and I do not serve! You shall never have her, Tom Jones. She has been carried off by her father to marry a toad named Blifil.

(She faints again.)

TOM. *(Heartbroken:)* Blifil.

(He exits. SOPHIA now sits on a simple country chair, while WESTERN kneels beside her.)

SQUIRE WESTERN. You will be the death of your poor father at last, my girl. Come, do consent to have un an thou shalt have the finest jewels and a coach and six at your command. Odrabbitit! I had rather hear your voice than the music of the best pack of dogs in England. I have no other comfort on earth but thee Sophy.

SOPHIA. Indeed, my dear papa, I know you have loved me tenderly. If it will content you, I will give the most solemn promise not to marry at all while my papa lives.

SQUIRE WESTERN. *(Pounding the floor in frustration:)* 'Tis neither here nor there Sophy! Damn me to the eternal fire but I am determined on this match!

(SOPHIA bursts out in a flood of tears.)

Cocks and pox, but I shall fall into fits at this weeping!

(He stamps out. SOPHIA moves to one side of the stage. TOM enters at the other. Each speaks a letter while the other reads it.)

TOM. Madam, pardon me the presumption if I ask you whether my advice, my assistance, my presence, my absence, my death, or my tortures can bring you any relief? I can only offer the most perfect admiration, the most ardent love, the most melting tenderness, the most resigned submission to your will, to make amends for my failings and mistakes. Forgive me if you can. Accept me if you will. My only wish is to see you every moment the happiest of women, or if not, to hear you are so. But no misery on earth can equal mine while I think you owe an uneasy moment to him who is, madam, in every sense and to every purpose, your devoted, Thomas Jones.

SOPHIA. *(She speaks, he reads:)* Sir, I can only offer the firm persuasion that you must divert your thought from what fortune hath, I fear, made impossible. I charge you to write me no more—at present at least; perhaps our fate will be at some time kinder to us both than at present. Believe this, I shall always think of you and am, sir, your humble servant, Sophia Western.

(*Both exit.* MISS WESTERN, *the Squire's sister, enters and so does he.*)

WESTERN. Zounds and the devil! Do you not commend me for what I have done?

MISS WESTERN. To lock up your daughter? Women in a free country are not to be treated so. Set her at liberty this instant!

WESTERN. Is there a hell besides women?! (*Tosses her the key:*) Do as you will.

MISS WESTERN. My will is this, brother, she shall be committed wholly and without meddling to my care.

WESTERN. Take the undutiful wench!

MISS WESTERN. I will. You reek of spirits, sir.

(*Lights change. Two chairs.* SOPHIA *and* MISS WESTERN *sit.*)

SOPHIA. I decline Mr. Jones' entreaties as it is against father's wishes.

MISS WESTERN. But you care for him?

SOPHIA. I cannot say.

MISS WESTERN. Think thou I have not lived?

(SOPHIA *exits.* LADY BELLASTON *sits with* MISS WESTERN.)

LADY BELLASTON. I wonder not that the girl's head is turned, as Jones, I am told, is a very agreeable fellow.

MISS WESTERN. As agreeable, I am sure, as this Blifil is hideous.

LADY BELLASTON. Further, it is said, he possesses the one virtue which men say is a great recommendation to us.

MISS WESTERN. It is very warm.

LADY BELLASTON. It will amuse you, I think, to hear the fellow had the assurance to make love to me. Including, with an effrontery I cannot dismiss, a proposal of marriage.

(*She exits.* SOPHIA *sits. Lights change.*)

SOPHIA. This...I can hardly believe...can it be true?

MISS WESTERN. A great lady would not deign to fabricate such a tale. What reason would she have?

SOPHIA. Can I have been so mistaken in him?

MISS WESTERN. Poor girl. Pray, take my handkerchief.

> *(They exit. A street.* TOM *enters one way and* MRS. FITZPAT-RICK *another.)*

MRS. FITZPATRICK. Mr. Jones.

TOM. Mrs. Fitzpatrick.

WOMAN 4. There are some women with whom self is so predominant that they never detach it from any subject. Thus the more Tom poured out his love and praise of Sophia, the more Mrs. Fitzpatrick, hearing of Sophia's beauty, wit, and gentility found her only thought was how much more praise she herself deserved.

MRS. FITZPATRICK. I must say, Mr. Jones, that any woman that makes no return to such a passion and such a person, is unworthy of both. Find me at home tomorrow and there shall be…remedy.

> *(She exits.* MR. FITZPATRICK *enters with* MRS. WATERS *on his arm.)*

TOM. Mr. Fitzpatrick, Mrs. Waters!

MR. FITZPATRICK. Have you, sir, been tête a tête with my wife?

TOM. How glad I am to see you both.

MR. FITZPATRICK. What business had you with my wife!

MRS. WATERS. Your business now, James, is with me.

TOM. Good friends, I hope no ill blood now remains upon some small mistakes made so long ago at Upton?

MR. FITZPATRICK. At Upton, no, I will drink a bottle with you presently, but first I will give you a great knock upon your pate.

> *(He does.)*

MRS. WATERS. Courtesy, James.

MR. FITZPATRICK. Well?

TOM. I grant you the blow, friend.

MR. FITZPATRICK. Do you friend?

> *(Does it again.)*

TOM. But not that one, sir.

MR. FITZPATRICK. *(He draws.)* You will, I hope, forgive me if I kill you.

> *(TOM draws, they fight.)*

MRS. WATERS. You must stop gentlemen. We are seen.

(TOM stabs FITZPATRICK. *He steps back and bows.)*

MR. FITZPATRICK. I have satisfaction enough. I am a dead man.

(He falls. MRS. WATERS *runs to him and kneels.* TOM *approaches. She looks up at him and shakes her head. A whistle sounds.)*

MRS. WATERS. Run Tom, or you will be taken.

(He exits. Lights change. FITZPATRICK *is dragged off,* MRS. WATERS *following.* SOPHIA *and* MISS WESTERN *cross the stage talking as a table and three chairs are set downstage.)*

MISS WESTERN. The proposal of Mr. Jones to Lady Bellaston makes clear the misdirection of your heart.

SOPHIA. I cannot understand, but what more surprises me is that he would do so at the very time he had such concern on my account?

(They exit. BLIFIL, ALLWORTHY, *and* WESTERN *sit.)*

BLIFIL. Killed him in the street, sir, as a common murderer might. He is arrested and remanded to Southwork prison where he awaits the rope.

WESTERN. There Squire, clear as glass. I say let the son of a whore of a bastard of somebody's, I know not whose, go to an unmarked grave and give the girl to Blifil here.

ALLWORTHY. We must hear this from her, Western, and no one else. *(Exits.)*

WESTERN. Hah! *(Slaps* BLIFIL *on the back.)* Two great estates made one, eh? And the girl full succulent into the bargain.

ALLWORTHY. *(Returns with* SOPHIA.*)* Now then, my good girl, Blifil is proposed but only you may put the stamp on it.

WESTERN. To the oars, cocksman.

BLIFIL. Most esteemed and honored lady, if I may enumerate the Christian principles, from which or I might say owing to which, I regard you as…

WESTERN. Kiss her, idiot!

*(*BLIFIL *clumsily kisses* SOPHIA. *She slaps him and runs off.)*

WESTERN. After her sir, hounds to the scent! *(A pause and then* BLIFIL *exits in the other direction.)* Fled like wounded ferret.

MAID. Lady to see you, sir.

*(*MRS. WATERS *enters.)*

MRS. WATERS. Is it so long, sir, that you do not recollect me?

SQUIRE WESTERN and ALLWORTHY. *Jenny Jones!*

MRS. WATERS. As was, sir. I'm Mrs. Waters now and I lodge with a Mr. Fitzpatrick, abandoned by his wife, and nurse the poor gentleman back to health after a duel was fought between himself and Tom Jones, well known to you.

WESTERN. What? The man he murdered?

MRS. WATERS. No murder with the murdered alive, eh? He says clear he provoked Mr. Jones, is the truth of it.

ALLWORTHY. I knew the boy was no villain!

WESTERN. But do they not hang him, madam?

MRS. WATERS. Tomorrow afternoon, Squire.

ALLWORTHY. But this Fitzpatrick must show himself to the magistrate.

MRS. WATERS. He cannot, sir, rise from his bed. And a common woman, such as myself cannot gain admittance to the court.

WESTERN. I will drag this Fitzpatrick to the prison gate and boot him 'til he speaks. I'll home for sword and pistol, for though the boy is a poacher and a scoundrel he shall not hang for a crowd of London fops! *(Exits.)*

MRS. WATERS. I've particular business with you Squire Allworthy.

ALLWORTHY. Quickly then.

MRS. WATERS. You gave poor Tom my maiden name of Jones but it was not deserved. Do you recall of a young fellow the name of Summer?

ALLWORTHY. Son of a clergyman of great learning and virtue. So it was the son there.

MRS. WATERS. No, it was the clergyman.

ALLWORTHY. I stand amazed! And you the mother?

MRS. WATERS. No sir. Though it's true these hands conveyed the fault to your bed, it was your sister was the mother of the child.

ALLWORTHY. I need not, madam, express astonishment. My sister did often seek out Pastor Summer for…instruction. And surely there is no benefit for you to express an untruth.

MRS. WATERS. She was highly rejoiced her plot had so well succeeded.

ALLWORTHY. Tom is then my own dear nephew, rightly my heir, and falsely accused of murder! *(Embraces* MRS. WATERS.*)* Dear woman. I must to Sophia and then Squire Western that we may not be too late to save him. Come, come.

(ALLWORTHY *enters to* SOPHIA.)

Tom Jones who has long loved you, he is my nephew. I shall never be able to reward him for his suffering without your assistance. Say you see in him the good qualities that will make him a husband?

SOPHIA. At present, sir, there is not a man upon the earth whom I would more resolutely reject than Mr. Jones. He has proved himself more variable than May weather.

ALLWORTHY. But…

SQUIRE WESTERN. (*Offstage:*) Arm, Allworthy, arm! We may arrive too late!

(SOPHIA, *handkerchief to her eyes, runs off one way,* ALLWORTHY *the other. A hangman's noose drops in and it is fitted round* TOM's *neck as he stands on a hay bale by a 'HANGMAN.' A bench is aced downstage and* LADY BELLASTON *enters.*)

LADY BELLASTON. Good morning.

TOM. Lady Bellaston! Have you come to save me?

LADY BELLASTON. (*Moving down to the bench:*) I have come to watch you dance on air, Tom Jones.

(*She sits, facing up.*)

HANGMAN. Thus convicted of the public murder of one James Fitzpatrick, Thomas Jones, parents unknown, shall this day be hanged by the neck until dead by magistrate's order.

(*Lights down on* TOM *as* ALLWORTHY *and* WESTERN *'ride' to his rescue.*)

WESTERN. Odzookers, neighbor Allworthy, you don't know what it is to govern a daughter. She shall marry young Tom and our estates together shall rival any and all. Ride hard, sir, it does no good, oddsrabbitit, to cut down a bridegroom who's dead as a turnip!

(*They ride off. We cut back to* TOM. *The* HANGMAN *stands next to him.*)

HANGMAN. Have you aught to say in your final moment?

TOM. Only the hope that my one love Sophia may find in memory some good in me.

(SQUIRE WESTERN *with sword in one hand, pistol in the other, enters firing.* ALLWORTHY *follows, also armed.*)

SQUIRE WESTERN. *(Plays the audience as his enemy:)* Hold you turd-beetles, you scum of Satan! Back! *(Turns to drive off the HANGMAN.)* I'll swinge thee till there be fountains scarlet and carpets of the dead!

> *(WESTERN slashes and fires downstage while ALLWORTHY cuts TOM loose. He falls to the floor, rope still around his neck. WESTERN grabs the cut end and with TOM holding the noose still around his neck, drags TOM offstage saying:)*

I have you now, sir, and you shall marry my daughter or by God sir, I shall hang you myself!

LADY BELLASTON. *(As she leaves:)* Ah well, it remains my opinion that marriage and hanging are very much the same.

> *(She exits. Two chairs are set quite a distance apart. TOM sits in one and SOPHIA the other. During the scene they move their chairs toward each other.)*

SOPHIA. You are most fortunate, sir, in the discovery of your birth.

TOM. How, fortunate? When I have incurred your displeasure?

SOPHIA. You must pass judgment on your own conduct.

TOM. It is mercy and not judgment I implore.

SOPHIA. Must I mention Lady Bellaston?

TOM. To propose marriage to the lady was the only way to end her pursuit of me.

SOPHIA. And the amour at the Inn at Upton while I fancied your heart to be mine? What happiness might I assure with a man capable of such inconstancy?

TOM. Had I hopes I might be yours, I could never have been another's. *(On his knees:)* No repentance was ever more sincere, name any proof within my power? *(Moves her downstage to an imaginary mirror. Stands behind her.)* Behold your grace. Those eyes, their shape and the pure mind shining through them. Can the man so reflected be inconstant? I cannot bear the burden of your silence.

> *(Starts away.)*

SOPHIA. Wait.

> *(He turns.)*

If I could forgive, I cannot trust. Your retention sir, must submit to time's own test.

TOM. Such trial I embrace. A day? A week?

SOPHIA. A twelvemonth, perhaps.

       (TOM falls to the floor as if shot.)

TOM. You have named eternity.

SOPHIA. Then one day less.

TOM. Whatever the trial, I must, I will thank those dear lips which sweetly have pronounced my hope.

       (He kisses her. After a moment she responds. SQUIRE WESTERN enters.)

WESTERN. Zoodikers! The marriage shall be tomorrow!

SOPHIA. One day less than a year, sir.

WESTERN. A year my ass! *(To TOM:)* I thought you a lad of higher mettle than to give way to parcel of maidenly flim-flam. I have seen you at it, girl!

SOPHIA. But father, you have forbid it.

WESTERN. Ha! When I forbade him you whined and languished. Now I am for him, you are against him. It is only to disoblige and contradict me.

SOPHIA. What would my papa have me do?

WESTERN. This! *(Puts her hand in TOM's.)* And consent, Lady Contrary, to tomorrow morning.

       (A pause.)

SOPHIA. I must be obedient to you father.

TOM. And I to you, mistress.

       (WESTERN capers around the room.)

WESTERN. Ha, ha! Done and done! Damn me if he shan't be tousling the wench! Where the devil is Allworthy!

       (TOM and SOPHIA kiss.)

Suck my honeybees, suck!

       (Exits.)

Allworthy!

SOPHIA. With that kiss we are betrothed, sir.

TOM. Oh, my angel, how may I thank your goodness?

SOPHIA. Our lives are in your power.

TOM. And all that I hope, in yours.

       (ALLWORTHY and WESTERN enter.)

WESTERN. Tell, Sophy, has not given thy consent to be married tomorrow?

SOPHIA. I dare not, sir, be guilty of disobedience.

WESTERN. See sir, what a father's authority is?

ALLWORTHY. I hope there is not the least constraint.

SOPHIA. I do not repent, nor shall I ever, a promise to Mr. Jones.

WESTERN. Kiss again, squirrels! Show the Squire how thou dost press together!

(They do.)

Constraint my nub, sir! Harkee, Allworthy, I'll wager five pounds to a crown we cradle a boy tomorrow, nine months!

(Music plays. WESTERN *begins a dance with* ALLWORTHY, TOM *with* SOPHIA, *and the rest the cast joins in. Lights down.)*

End of Play

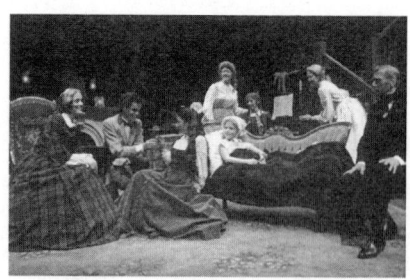